The Captive Skylark Or Do As You Would Be Done By: A Tale

Clara De Chatelain

In the interest of creating a more extensive selection of rare historical book reprints, we have chosen to reproduce this title even though it may possibly have occasional imperfections such as missing and blurred pages, missing text, poor pictures, markings, dark backgrounds and other reproduction issues beyond our control. Because this work is culturally important, we have made it available as a part of our commitment to protecting, preserving and promoting the world's literature. Thank you for your understanding.

THE CAPTIVE SKY-LARK;

OR,

DO AS YOU WOULD BE DONE BY.

A Tale.

BY

MADAME DE CHATELAIN.

LONDON: JAMES HOGG & SONS.

As the fresh Rose-bud needs the silvery shower,
  The golden sunshine, and the pearly dew,
  The joyous day with all its changes new,
Ere it can bloom into the perfect flower ;
So with the human rose-bud ; from sweet airs
  Of heaven will fragrant purity be caught,
  And influences benign of tender thought
Inform the soul, like angels, unawares.

MARY HOWITT.

Algernon caged. P. 51.

The Captive Sky-lark.

CONTENTS.

THE CAPTIVE SKY-LARK; OR, DO AS YOU WOULD BE DONE BY—

	PAGE
CHAPTER I.	7
CHAPTER II.	21
CHAPTER III.	39
CHAPTER IV.	59
CHAPTER V.	81
CHAPTER VI.	101

THE CAPTIVE SKY-LARK;

OR,

DO AS YOU WOULD BE DONE BY.

CHAPTER I.

A LITTLE lark sat in a cage that was hanging outside a pretty house in the country. There was a smooth lawn reaching up to the parlour windows, dotted with what appeared like baskets of beautiful flowers lying on the grass—only they were really growing—besides clumps of trees affording a welcome shade, and a rose-tree that covered the wall of the house up to the first floor. The weather, too, was bright and balmy, and everything looked gladsome; but what was all this to the lark? He was a prisoner, and it mattered little to him that his cage was handsome, for it was a prison just the same. And what cared he for the delightful garden, or even the summer weather, when he was not free to fly about to enjoy it? He who was accustomed to fly up—up—in the vast expanse of the open air, would now have knocked his head—poor bird!—if he had followed the instinct of soaring within the narrow precincts of his prison, which was not even a proper lark's cage, with a cloth top. But he attempted no such thing, any more than he thought of singing—and there he sat, gloomy and disconsolate, as though he were pining to death for want of liberty.

Now, if any compassionate little readers should ask who was cruel enough to confine the poor lark in a cage, we shall inform them that the diminutive tyrant who bereft a helpless, dumb creature of its freedom, was no bigger than themselves, but was a pretty little girl, about seven years old, whose rosy cheeks and fair locks were the admiration of everybody, when she appeared in her nice white frock and blue sash, in her mamma's drawing-room. Yet Cecily had not exactly a bad heart; but she was selfish and wilful; and as her mother, through indolence, brought on by ill-health, indulged all her whims, in order to keep her quiet, the little lady, of course, profited by her parent's weakness, and had no notion of being contradicted. Thus one day she longed for a poodle, and accordingly a poodle was bought, and was a favourite for a few weeks, until she beat him, and he growled and threatened to bite, when she declared he was a "nasty" dog, and he was forbidden the house. Then she took a fancy to have a bird, and it must be a lark. So a lark was purchased, and put into a cage to please her; and then in a few days' time, Cecily thought no more about the lark, who might have died of hunger and thirst if she had had the care of feeding him. Only she never thought of setting him free for all that—Oh no!

She ran about the garden herself, and jumped about, and enjoyed the fresh air, and the smell of the flowers, and would have thought it very hard if she had been kept only half an hour indoors against her will; but she cared nothing for what the lark might feel or suffer. Cecily was in truth a most selfish little girl.

The house inhabited by Cecily's mother, was situated next door to a very pretty cottage, whose grounds were only separated from her garden by an invisible fence. The cottage happened to be let that year to a family from London, consisting of a lady and her two children, who came down into the country for a change of air.

The very next morning Cecily happened

to see her two new little neighbours playing at the flying circle, which they threw to each other, and caught on a couple of sticks with great spirit and dexterity. The children were playing with a hearty enjoyment quite pleasing to behold. After watching their game for awhile, Cecily called out to them in her small, shrill voice, saying: "Come and play with me in our garden."

Algernon and Rosina now approached the edge of the ha-ha on the other side of the fence, to hear what their new acquaintance said to them; but when they found what she wanted, they said they must ask leave first, and their mamma was not yet up.

"I never ask leave for anything," said Cecily."

"Oh, how naughty!" cried Rosina.

"Do lend me a pair of sticks, and let's play over the fence," persisted Cecily.

So to oblige her, Algernon ran down into the ha-ha, and gave her a pair of sticks through the fence, and began to play with her; but Cecily missed the hoop so many times, that she soon threw up the game in disgust, and returned the sticks, though she still lingered near the fence to talk to her little neighbours. She asked them their names, their ages, what playthings they had, and all such questions as children ask of each other.

Rosina was just the same age as herself, though smaller and more timid-looking; while Algernon, who was about two years older, was a very fine little fellow, and looked as healthy as he was good-natured. After they had answered her questions, Cecily told them all about her own toys, and saying that she had besides, a live play thing, she ran and fetched the lark in his cage.

"Poor little thing!" said Rosina, "you should let him fly away."

"No, I won't," said Cecily, "he's mine."

"O fie!" cried Algernon, "how naughty papa and mamma would think you."

"I dont care," replied Cecily, "I shall do as I like."

The poodle, who had been given to the gardener, ever since he had offended Miss Cecily, now came running by, and began barking at the bird, and leaping up at the cage she held in her hand. The dog meant it only for play, but the poor lark, who could not understand his meaning, was frightened to death, and fluttered about the cage in an agony of terror. It was quite as alarming to him to see the dog's snout close to the bars of the cage, as a lion would be to us, if he suddenly peeped through a barred window, behind which we stood.

"Don't let the dog frighten the poor bird—pray, don't," said Rosina, entreatingly.

But Cecily only laughed, and kept twirling round, and bobbing the cage up and down, so as to excite the dog still more.

"Here—here," cried Algernon, whistling to the poodle, who soon wriggled through the fence, and came wagging his tail to bestow his caresses on his new acquaintance. He then darted off to scour the garden, forgetting the lark and everything else in his frolicsome mood.

"You are such a naughty little girl," said Algernon, "that we won't play with you any more."

So saying, he retired with his sister; and they amused themselves in a distant part of the garden, till breakfast time.

"O mamma," said the two children, "what a wicked little girl lives next door to us!"

"Hush, my dears!" replied their mother, "you should not call people wicked till you know more about them—and you've only seen this little girl once. But tell we what makes you think so ill of her?"

The children related what had past.

"It is plain she has been very badly brought up," said Mrs. Mildmay, "and not taught her duty towards animals. Let us hope, if she were reasoned with properly, that she might grow better."

"Won't you talk to her, mamma?" said Algernon.

"I must wait to see whether my interference is wished for," said the mother; "and, in the meantime, you were quite right, my dears," added she, kissing the children, "to refuse to play with her."

It was not long before a trifling circumstance brought the two mammas acquainted with each other.

We can hardly say whether Cecily had been most provoked or surprised by the reproof her little neighbours had given her. Unaccustomed as she was to be thwarted, she never imagined that she could be in the wrong, and her heart swelled with indignation on finding that the children persisted on avoiding her, by playing at a distance from the fence. As anything we are excluded from seems doubly valuable, Cecily only longed the more to play with her neighbours, just because they seemed averse to do so, and she daily watched them with envious eyes.

One day that they were playing at their favourite game of the flying circle,

DO AS YOU WOULD BE DONE BY. 19

Algernon happened to fling the hoop with a jerk which pitched it right over the fence. Cecily saw it fall, and was running to snatch it up, when the dog, whom the gardener had taught to fetch and carry, seized the hoop in his mouth, and would have scrambled through the fence, had not his little mistress come and wrenched it pettishly from him, and struck him, saying: "You shan't, you naughty dog."

The brother and sister, who had seen her ill-natured interference, now came within speaking distance, and said: "Please to return us our hoop."

"I shan't!" said Cecily, hugging the hoop, and moving away from the fence.

"But it is ours," cried Algernon,

"I don't care," retorted Cecily, disappearing among the trees.

The hoop was not of any value, still it was prettily covered with ribbon of bright colours; and any way, it prevented their going on with the game. The children went and complained to their mother of Cecily's behaviour.

Mrs. Mildmay immediately sent in a servant with a civil message, requesting the hoop might be returned, and apologising for her little boy's having unintentionally cast it into Mrs. Wilton's garden.

CHAPTER II.

It was naturally to be expected that the hoop would have been immediately returned, with an equally-civil message on the part of Mrs. Wilton. But, instead of that, the servant brought a very foolish one, to the effect that Miss Cecily had cried so much at being asked to give up the hoop, that her mamma hoped Mrs. Mildmay would excuse its being returned for the present.

Thinking it was not only silly, but downright wrong, to let so wayward a child be encouraged in her obstinacy,

Mrs. Mildmay at once determined to call upon her neighbour, and reason with her on the subject.

She found Mrs. Wilton reclining on the sofa.

After apologizing politely for her intrusion, Mrs. Mildmay at once entered upon the object of her visit, saying that it was not for the value of the hoop, but, she trusted, for a higher motive—namely, for the moral welfare of the child herself, that she had taken such a step.

Mrs. Wilton coloured exceedingly, and said in a languid tone: "You see, ma'am, I am poorly, and when little Cis gets into a passion, it agitates my nerves—so I hoped you would excuse our returning the toy to-day—I promise you to get it from her as soon as I can."

So because she had weak nerves, Mrs. Wilton allowed her child to keep what did not belong to her!

Thus thought Mrs. Mildmay. She, however, said with gentle firmness: "I fear, my good lady, if you let her take such habits at this early age, that you will have cause to repent later."

"What can I do?" said Mrs. Wilton, languidly; "I am an invalid, and I cannot bear noise. I must keep Cis quiet."

"But not surely by spoiling her for ever?" said Mrs. Mildmay.

The lady was silent.

"Am I, then, to understand," resumed

Mrs. Mildmay, "that I must go away without the toy?"

"Indeed, ma'am, I feel quite ashamed," replied Mrs. Wilton, again blushing deeply, "but if you will but have patience for a day or two, Cis will get tired of the new plaything—I'll send some other toys to your two little cherubs, that they will like still better."

"I am obliged to you, madam," said Mrs. Mildmay, rather coldly; "but I do not wish any such thing to be done. All we want is to recover our own."

"What can I do?" again asked Mrs. Wilton, in pitiable helplessness.

"Will you let me speak to the child myself?" said Mrs. Mildmay, "and I dare say she'll soon give it me back."

"Very gladly," replied the mother; "only I hope you won't make her cry—I can't bear scenes, Mrs. Mildmay—you see I'm so nervous."

Mrs. Wilton then rang and told the servant to fetch Miss Cecily. When the little girl came in, and found the next door lady, as she called her, she first stared in surprise, then looked a little abashed, and was just going to run out of the room, when her mamma said, in a coaxing tone: "Now, my darling, here's a lady come to see if my little Cissy is a good girl, and will be so kind as to give back the pretty hoop—and my Cissy will—won't she, lovey?"

"No, I won't," was the ungracious reply.

"Won't you, poppet?" said the mother, soothingly; "now do, and you shall have more jam than pudding to-day at dinner!"

Cecily's eyes brightened for a moment at this tempting prospect, when her mamma, concluding the victory was half gained, thought to add a crowning weight to the scale, by observing: "And then this lady will let you play with her nice children—I know she will—if you're good, and give up the hoop."

"With your leave, madam," interrupted Mrs. Mildmay, "I can't promise Miss Cecily any such thing, because I don't like my children to play with little girls that behave so rudely."

"I want to play with them—I will

play with them," screamed Cecily, beginning to cry.

"Not till you learn better manners, child," said Mrs. Mildmay, calmly.

"Now, don't cry, Cis," said Mrs. Wilton, folding the child to her bosom, "don't spoil that pretty face with crying; I daresay the lady will—only she says so because you have been naughty— you know you have, you little rogue," added she, smiling.

And she made a sign over Cecily's head, to Mrs. Mildmay, as much as to say: "Do help to appease her, by giving way to her wishes."

But Mrs. Mildmay remained firm, and replied: "No, she must be good before I allow any such thing."

After Cecily's passion had worked itself out by a violent fit of sobbing, she dried her eyes, and looking up to Mrs. Mildmay, inquired: "Shall I be good if I give up the hoop?"

"I don't call that being good, but merely doing your duty," answered Mrs. Mildmay.

This seemed very harsh to Mrs. Wilton, who always tried, though so vainly, to coax Cecily into good behaviour, and now thought she ought to be encouraged when she almost offered to do what was right. But on Cecily, Mrs. Mildmay's words produced the effect which firmness generally obtains over spoilt children—she instinctively felt that tears and stamping, which

Returning the Hoop.　　　P. 29.

The Captive Sky-lark.

always succeeded with her mother, would be wholly unavailing with the strange lady, and that she would only forfeit for ever the chance of being admitted to play with her little neighbours. And, acting upon this intuitive reasoning with the quick impulse of her age, she ran out of the room into the garden, and, snatching up the hoop, returned before the two mammas had had time to exchange a word, and silently put it into Mrs. Mildmay's hands.

"There's my queen!" cried the partial mother, in ecstacies at what she considered the most heroic abnegation on her child's part—and fearful lest her neighbour should not fully appreciate the merit of such a sacrifice, she added:

"Now, I'm sure the lady will think you a very good darling indeed."

Mrs. Mildmay could not help smiling at her excessive silliness, as she said: "Indeed, ma'am, I am not so apt to think children 'good darlings' merely for doing that which it would be highly blameable not to do. However, it is a step in the right direction, and I hope in time we shall grow wiser," added she, patting little Cecily's flaxen locks.

"Now let me go and play with your children," said Cecily.

"You forget 'If you please, ma'am,'" observed Mrs. Wilton.

"If you please, ma'am," repeated Cecily, roughly.

"No," said Mrs. Mildmay, "I have

already told you that I only allow good children to play with mine—but when I hear better accounts of you, and when you cease to throw stones over the fence, or to beat your poor dog, then, perhaps, I may let you come."

At the word "no," Cecily had already gone off into another fit of crying, which she, however, suddenly checked on recollecting that it would perhaps only lengthen the time of probation; and this was at least one useful lesson she learnt from Mrs. Mildmay's first visit.

"Pray come and see me again," said Mrs. Wilton, when that lady rose to go, "I shall esteem it a great favour—for a word from you will have more effect on

Cis, than if I were to talk all day long. And if you will but let her frequent your nicely-behaved children, I may hope for her improvement."

Mrs. Mildmay said she would be happy to repeat her visit, since it was agreeable, and then took her leave.

For several days after, Cecily took great pains to be what she considered "very good indeed," which consisted chiefly of abstaining from annoying her neighbours, or worrying the dog. As for the poor lark, he still sat in his cage looking out wistfully at the pretty landscape beyond the garden. Cecily would never have thought of freeing *him*, as the means of turning over a new leaf in her behaviour; neither did she cease to be turbulent and troublesome in-doors, though not quite so much so as before this salutary visit. With the tenacity of a headstrong disposition determined to carry its point, she thus managed to keep up such an outward show of improvement as induced Mrs. Mildmay to abridge the period of trial she had originally meant the wayward child to undergo, and to unlock the gates of the paradise she coveted.

Mrs. Mildmay, therefore, came and paid her neighbour a visit, and having told her she saw with pleasure that her little girl had behaved so much better of late, inquired whether she was equally good at home? Being answered by a more rapturous than truthful affirmative from the mother, who was far too desirous that Cecily should have the advantage of such well-behaved playmates, to raise any difficulties, Mrs. Mildmay took the little girl home with her, and introduced her to her own children.

Now, of course, it was not to be expected that Cecily should be all of a sudden so thoroughly reformed, that her wayward spirit would not peep out every now and then, even during the hour she spent with her new companions. For, as we have seen, her improvement was only outward, and put on for an especial purpose; and now that her end was gained, she took less trouble to conceal her natural bent. Accordingly, she quarrelled two or three times with

Algernon and Rosina, ran over the platbands, and began plucking the flowers in spite of their remonstrances, and was at last only stopped by the gardener's coming to their assistance, and lifting her up, in spite of her screaming and kicking, and threatening to lock her up in the tool-house.

On hearing the noise, Mrs. Mildmay came out to see what was the matter, when Cecily hastily flung away the flowers she was holding in her frock.

"Children," said Mrs. Mildmay, looking displeased, " have I not forbidden you to pluck the flowers?"

Rosina blushed, but said nothing, for she did not like to accuse her new playmate, and Algernon followed her example, although he looked angrily at Cecily.

"Dear me! ma'am," said the gardener, "it is'nt *our* children that have done the mischief—but little miss there, who kicks worse than any vicious horse."

"Fie! you naughty man!" began Cecily, pelting him with the flowers she had uprooted—when Mrs. Mildmay took her very quietly by the hand, saying: "I shall now send you back, child, since I find your pretended reform was only a trick to get admitted into my house."

A few weeks ago, Cecily would have burst into a violent fit of crying, if anybody had ventured to thwart her in such a manner; but knowing it was quite useless, she at once submitted, though very sulkily, and went away without saying good-bye to either of her little neighbours.

CHAPTER III.

It was some time before Mrs. Mildmay could be prevailed upon to admit Cecily again, especially as her children begged they might not be obliged to play with the rude little girl any more. But Mrs. Wilton sent so many conciliatory messages, making such abundant apologies for her child's past misdemeanors, and promises of future good behaviour, that Mrs. Mildmay was induced to give her another trial, out of sheer pity for the mismanaged little girl and her weak-minded mother.

This time Cecily behaved better, though more from fear of being turned out again, than from any worthier motive. After awhile, by dint of frequenting her little neighbours, she grew less imperious and uncivil, and learned not to snatch things out of her playmates' hands. This was something towards improvement, to be sure; still it was not enough. If self-interest had taught Cecily to mend her manners towards her playfellows, no such lesson had enforced on her mind the necessity of showing kindness towards the brute creation; and when the children one day took her with them to feed their guinea-pigs and rabbits, and a pretty tame goat, that would eat out of their hands, she frightened all their little favourites by plucking the goat's beard, pinching the rabbits' ears, and sousing one of the poor little piggies into a pail of water, in which he would have been drowned had not Algernon quickly flown to rescue him.

"You are so naughty, Cecily," said the children, "that we never can love you—and we will ask our mother not to let you come any more."

Cecily now began to cry.

"I will come—and you shall love me," roared the wayward child.

"You shan't hurt our animals," replied Algernon.

Cecily promised she never would again, provided they did not tell their mamma this time. But the right-minded Rosina observed, that she ought to treat animals well for their own sakes, as her parents had taught her to do, and not for fear they should tell of her.

"Will you love me if I don't hurt them any more?" asked Cecily.

"Yes," said Rosina, "only you must not beat your own dog either, nor frighten your poor little lark."

"What is that to you?" said the unfeeling child, "aren't they mine?"

Oh these miniature tyrants, who dare to call God's creatures *theirs* as an excuse for ill-using them!

On the children's telling their mamma how ill their little neighbour had behaved, Mrs. Mildmay said she must not be admitted to the poultry-yard any more, until she had had some talk with Cecily's mother. An opportunity soon occurred to bring in the subject; for as in pity to Mrs. Wilton's invalid state, Mrs. Mildmay frequently called upon her, she generally heard some complaints of Cecily's headstrong disposition from the sick lady, who suffered keenly from the evils she had so sillily brought upon herself.

Mrs. Wilton complained bitterly that Cecily frequently made such a noise in the room, when she was lying on the sofa, that she could obtain no rest.

"I don't wonder at it, my dear Madam," replied Mrs. Mildmay, "for Cecily strikes me as being a very heartless little girl. See how unkind she is towards all animals."

"Dear me," exclaimed Mrs. Wilton, rather selfishly, "what has that to do with the matter? She may be unkind to animals, and yet have some feeling for her own mother."

Mrs. Mildmay shook her head. "My good lady," said she, "according as we sow, we shall reap. If we do not train the infant mind to be kind to all living creatures—still more, if we allow a child to vent its whims and love of power on dumb animals—that child will soon become hardened to all good feeling; and how can we expect it to show affection and duty to ourselves, when we have not taught it one of its important duties towards God?"

Mrs. Wilton looked up in surprise;

for she had never considered the matter in this light. She, however, hastened to say that she had never authorized Cecily to be unkind to any animal—Oh, no!—she was quite sure of that."

"Yet you allow her to keep that lark confined in a cage?" objected Mrs. Mildmay.

Mrs. Wilton coloured slightly at such a home argument, and tried to excuse herself on the plea, that "children must have play-things to amuse them," and that "one can't refuse them such a harmless wish as that of having a little pet," and so forth. She, however, concluded by saying that, if it would oblige Mrs. Mildmay, she would tell one of the servants to open the bird's cage as if by accident, and that Cecily need not know how it came by its liberty.

But Mrs. Mildmay said—" No; it would be far preferable to lead Cecily to open the cage of her own accord. If she missed the bird suddenly, she would only crave for some piping bullfinch or linnet to make a prisoner of in its stead —and that would be but a change of evil."

Mrs. Wilton's head sunk back on the cushions of the sofa, as if oppressed by the weight of thought her neighbour's remarks had called forth. She felt it quite impossible she could ever lead Cecily to do any such thing as open the lark's cage; and after remaining in perplexed silence for several minutes, she at length drawled out—"Tell me, Mrs. Mildmay, did your children never wish to have a bird in a cage?"

"Yes," replied Mrs. Mildmay, "Algernon was once set upon having a dove."

"And how did you manage to persuade him out of it?" inquired Mrs. Wilton.

"Very easily," answered Mrs. Mildmay. "His father said to him: 'Algernon, you shall have the dove, but on condition of spending a whole day just in the same way as your dove will have to live in his cage.'"

"What an odd idea!" cried Mrs. Wilton, who now rose up from the cushions, and began to feel interested.

"And did the little fellow accept the proposal?"

"To be sure he did," continued Mrs. Mildmay. "We were residing at that time in a very nice cottage we had taken for the season, in Devonshire, and there happened to be a very pretty summer-house in the garden; and into this summer-house Master Algernon was conveyed early in the morning of the day he was to spend like a bird in a cage."

"Was he locked in?" inquired Mrs. Wilton.

"Of course he was," answered Mrs. Mildmay. "Breakfast was put ready for him, and when we left him to go and take our more social meal, he was in very high spirits. He thought it would be so pleasant to be in the summer-house all day long, and not have any lessons to attend to, and only to read the story-books which were left for his use, and look out at the pretty garden. After breakfast, his little sister came and asked him how he liked being a bird? And he popped his little head out of the window, and assured her he liked it vastly, and didn't care how long it lasted. By and bye his papa and I walked past the window, when he asked us to lift little Rosina into the summer-house to play with him. But we told him that would never do— and that he must be alone in his cage, just as the dove was to be."

"I should never have had the heart to refuse the dear little fellow," interrupted Mrs. Wilton.

"Well, we thought differently," continued Mrs. Mildmay, smiling; "and we had even the heart to add that we were going to take her out with us for a drive in the pony-chaise. Poor little Algey then looked half sorrowful, and said he should have liked to go too. 'But, Algey, my boy!' said his father, 'you forget that you are to behave like a bird to-day—and birds don't ride in carriages.' 'But birds fly, papa,' objected Algernon. 'So they do, my dear, when they are not in a cage,' replied we. Algernon had nothing more to say. 'Now, good-bye, Algernon,' said his papa, 'you shall be duly fed—never fear.'"

"And did you really leave him locked in—poor little man?" asked Mrs. Wilton.

"Certainly we did," replied Mrs. Mildmay, "but he was not quite lonely either; for Rosina begged so hard to be left at home to take care of her 'bird,' as she called her brother, that we did not like to refuse her. And she gathered flowers for him, which she threw in at the window, for she was not tall enough to reach up to it; and I believe they even played at ball, as well as they could under the circumstances.

"When the children's dinner-hour came, the servant brought Master Algernon his meal, as she had been told to do, and put in the tray at the window,—grumbling, however, that the young gentleman was not being fed like a Christian. Presently we came home, bringing with us two children belonging to a neighbour, who often played with our little ones, and took them into the garden, and made them over to Rosina, who was loitering about near the summer-house. We then went to see Algernon. 'Well, boy,' said papa, 'do you still like your cage?' 'Yes, papa,' said Algey, though not so briskly as in the morning; and he showed us the flowers his sister had brought him, and told us he had still some stories to read. 'I see that you'll win the dove, Algey, my boy,' said his father; and thereupon we left him."

"I should have given it him at once," cried Mrs. Wilton; "but go on, for I long to know how you got out of the scrape, and disappointed the poor little fellow of his bird, which I am sure you did, you naughty woman."

"Why, by and by, Algernon heard the voices of the two children, playing with Rosina," resumed Mrs. Mildmay, "when he shouted out to them to come and play near the summer-house, that he might profit by their company. Edgar and Harry then asked Rosina if her brother was naughty that he was shut up in the summer-house? But when they learnt how matters stood, they came and laughed at him, and pelted him in his cage, till Algey began to grow vexed, and would probably have quarrelled with them, had not some new freak called off the children's attention and made them scamper away in another direction. Algernon looked after them, and longed to run too, and when he heard his sister's joyous laugh as she pursued the little boys, and caught a last glimpse of her frock as she disappeared behind the trees, he began to feel rather lonely. Soon after, the clouds that had been gathering since noon, fell down in a heavy shower, and Rosina, with her little companions, were obliged to take refuge in the house, where they played at all sorts of indoor games. When the rain had ceased, Edgar and Harry returned home, while Rosina stole out into the wet garden, and ran to see after Algernon. Poor little fellow! The shower had completely matured all his reflections on the evils of captivity, which the timely visit of his little playmates had first awakened, and he begged his sister not to lose a minute, but to run back to the house, and tell papa and mamma that he would give up the dove, and only asked to be let out. His trusty little messenger soon brought us word of what he wished, and his papa immediately proceeded to the summer-house and unlocked the door.

"Now, you must remember, Algernon," said he, "that if you cross the threshold, you lose all claim to the dove."

"Yes, papa," replied Algernon, "but I no longer wish for one."

"Why not, my boy?" said his father.

"Because," returned Algernon, "I've been thinking it would be very dull for the poor dove to be shut up in a cage, since I don't like being locked up here—and yet it's not so bad for me either, as it would be for the dove."

"Why do you think so, my child?" asked papa.

"You know, papa, the dove can't read books as I can," answered Algernon, "and then it wants to fly, and that must be worse than my wanting to run after Edgar and Harry."

"Rightly reasoned, my little fellow," said his father, kissing him; "I have no fear now to let you come out."

And I assure you that, from that day,

Algernon never again expressed the slightest wish for confining a bird in a cage."

Mrs. Wilton had listened with intense interest to this little account, and when her neighbour had ceased speaking, she said, with a sigh: "I wish Cecily were only half as good as your children. But if I had shut *her* up in that manner, she would have broken the door open, or thrown the chairs out of the window— and then have wanted the bird all the same."

"Which you would, no doubt, have given her," observed Mrs. Mildmay, with a quiet smile.

Although too supine to profit by the advice she had often received from her neighbour, yet the frequency of similar conversations, and still more a slight improvement in the manners of her wayward child, since she was allowed to frequent the little Mildmays, had at least the effect of convincing Mrs. Wilton that her mode of education had hitherto proved very inefficient; and she began secretly to rejoice at the wholesome control that Mrs. Mildmay exercised over Cecily, during the hours she spent at that lady's house.

CHAPTER IV.

CECILY had been forbidden to repeat her visit to the poultry-yard, a prohibition she had borne unmurmuringly, although frequently vexed when either of the children went in to feed the animals, and she was obliged to remain in the garden. But she had learnt that Mrs. Mildmay's laws were not to be infringed, and being very much set upon obtaining leave to enter once more the forbidden precincts, just because they *were* forbidden, she had found out that the best way of gaining her ends would be to seem to have grown very good. Now it was not right in Cecily to aim merely at *seeming* to be good; she ought to have tried to be so in right earnest. However, even the habit of trying to seem so, proved a salutary one, for she found it much easier to be kind and gentle with her playmates than she could have imagined. And then she began to feel a secret pride in showing Mrs. Mildmay that she could be good if she chose; for, strange to say, spoilt and wayward as she was, the slightest word of approval from that lady was more gratifying to her than all the silly praises that were lavished upon her at home.

While this silent change was beginning to be effected in Cecily's manners, her mother's health had grown worse, and the doctor ordered her removal to the sea-side for a change of air.

Mrs. Wilton was puzzled what to do with Cecily.

"For," said she to Mrs. Mildmay, with whom she had now grown intimate, "Cecily will grow very fidgetty at being cooped up in a lodging-house. And if *she* is fidgetty there's no quiet to be had in the house—and I require rest. What had I better do? Do you advise me to send her to school?"

Mrs. Mildmay reflected for a few minutes, and then said, that if Mrs. Wilton liked, she would take charge of Cecily during her absence, but it must be on one condition—namely, that she were entirely given over to her guidance, just as if she were one of her own children.

"On any condition you please, my dear Mrs. Mildmay," cried Mrs. Wilton, joyfully, "and I wish in my heart that she may grow more like any child of yours."

Accordingly, Mrs. Wilton set off on her journey shortly afterwards, and Cecily was taken to her new home.

Cecily was at first amazingly delighted at the idea that she should now play all day long in the garden with the little Mildmays, instead of only going in for an hour or so. She was therefore rather disappointed when she found that they had lessons to attend to, and that the whole day was not made up of play.

"How idle you must be, Cecily," said Rosina; "why, Algey and I always play much better after having done our work."

"I shall allow Cecily a holiday for the first three days, till she learns our ways," said Mrs. Mildmay; "but after that she must do something, or else she will not be allowed to play with you at your recreation time."

And then Cecily was told to leave the school-room, as the children must not be disturbed at their lessons, and to run about the garden as she pleased, provided she did no mischief.

Cecily was, however, soon tired of running about, and she came every now and then up to the study window, to see if her playmates had finished attending to their "tiresome books," as she called them. But the children were busy at their tasks, and Mrs. Mildmay took no more notice of her than if she had not seen her. Nor had she the resource of teasing her favourite maid, who had been trained to gratify all her whims, for she was gone to the sea-side to nurse her sick mamma; and Mrs. Mildmay's maid would not let her into the poultry-yard, though Cecily said, " I will go,"—all of which ruffled her sadly.

At last Cecily bethought her that she had one animal whom she could feed— for the lark had been brought into Mrs. Mildmay's garden—and so she went and begged some barley-meal and water-cresses of the cook, and put them into the little captive's cage, and filled his glass with some nice, cool water, and then proceeded to hang some flowers and leaves over the cage to make a kind of bower of it.

And the poor little lark uttered a faint tweat! tweat! in a grateful, though mournful tone, as if to thank her for her attentions.

It was all very well to deck his cage, but it would have been better still to have given him his freedom, to seek the green nooks no cage can replace. However, it was something that Cecily thought of trying to make him more comfortable, and she was rewarded for it by seeing him peck at the water-cresses with great delight; and for the first time in her life, she felt a degree of pleasure at having contributed to the comfort of a living creature.

"O, how smart you have made his cage!" cried little Algernon, who came running across the lawn, as the hour for play had now struck.

"And he'll be so nice and cool," observed Rosina, joining them in turn.

"Wouldn't you like to have a bird?" asked Cecily.

"O, we have plenty of birds," replied the children, "and we'll show them to you if you'll promise not to frighten them."

Cecily said she would not, and then Rosina ran and fetched a little basket, and they all three struck across a path leading to the outskirts of the garden, and, having crossed a style, found themselves in a pretty grove that Cis had not yet seen.

"But I don't see any cages," said the little girl, "where are your birds?"

"We'll call them in a minute," answered Algernon.

They had now approached a circular spot, which resembled a kind of natural pavilion, with the trees arching over head, when the two children began to make a chirping noise.

This language seemed to be understood by the feathered inhabitants of the neighbouring trees, for whole flocks of birds answered the call, like the gathering of clans at the sound of their chieftain's bugle.

"O, what a pretty sight!" exclaimed Cecily, running towards the birds, who immediately took wing in great alarm.

"You must keep still, Cecily," said Rosina, "for they are frightened at the sight of a stranger;" and she told her to stand behind, till the birds grew used to her.

So Cecily did as she was bid, because she wanted the birds to return, and presently they came back; and though at first they looked round warily, before they picked up the seed the children flung them, and then snatched it hastily and retreated, they grew bolder by degrees; and finding that the object of their terror (namely, Cecily) remained quite still, they at last hopped about

Feeding the Birds. P. 68.

The Captive Skylark.

after their usual familiar fashion, sometimes up to the children's feet, sometimes perching on their shoulders.

When the contents of the basket were emptied, the children said it was time to return.

"Will you let me help to feed the birds next time?" asked Cecily, eagerly.

The children said she should as soon as ever the birds had grown used to her.

"And will they grow to love me, too?" inquired Cecily.

"They'll soon love anybody that feeds them," said Algernon.

"And that does not hurt them," added Rosina.

Wisdom itself could not have devised

a more sensible answer, than natural good feeling suggested to these two children.

The children returned to their lessons, while Cecily fetched her doll, and sat on a bench in the garden, dressing and undressing her mimic baby, and looking every five minutes towards the windows of the room where her playmates were performing their little tasks, and longing for them to come out again. Then she jumped up, and began throwing stones into the brook running through the garden, till she splashed herself from head to foot; and next she thought she would give dolly a bath, since mamma was gone to the sea-side to bathe—only as dolly was made of wax, the bath did not improve her beauty, and Cecily was so disappointed at the results, that she flung her down on the grass, calling her a " naughty doll."

Presently she picked the doll up again, and finding it still too wet to put on its clothes, she climbed on to the bench under the tree where the lark's cage was hanging, and said to the lark : " Look at the " nasty doll."

The doll's head put close to the wires of the cage was about as alarming to the poor bird as Gog and Magog in the Lord Mayor's procession might be to some little child three years old, if either of these worthies were to peep in at the first-floor window. He fluttered about anxiously from his perch to the floor, in his endeavours to retreat as far as possible from the object of his terror. But this was amusement to Cecily, who laughed aloud at his panic, and began tearing down the pretty foliage she had put round his cage a few hours before, saying: " You *shall* look at the nasty doll."

While she was thus notably employed, the two children came out of the school-room, accompanied by Mrs. Mildmay.

At the sight of the latter, Cecily blushed deeply, and hastily jumped down from the bench.

" What are you doing, Cecily?" said Mrs. Mildmay, in a tone of displeasure.

Cecily stammered, looked foolish, and hung down her head.

"I had begun to think better of you,

Cecily, this morning, on seeing you deck your bird's cage," said Mrs. Mildmay, but I'm afraid you'll never learn to do as you would be done by."

A few tears had gathered in Cecily's eyes, and now began to steal down her cheeks. This time, however, she did not cry from passion, but because she began to feel really sorry that Mrs. Mildmay could so seldom think her good long together, and she said, in a very penitent tone: "I'll make him another nice arbour, ma'am, if you'll let me."

"Well, child, we will take care of that," said Mrs. Mildmay, "for you must go and change your shoes and stockings, as I see you have been getting into the wet. As for your doll, she's quite spoilt, and I shall ask your mamma not to let you have another, till you learn how to take care of it."

Mrs. Mildmay had seen from the window the foolish way in which the little girl filled up her idle moments, but had not interfered, thinking it was well worth the loss of a plaything to give her a good lesson; and only interposed her authority when she saw her annoying the bird.

Cecily was glad to slink away; and when her clothes had been changed, she played quietly in the house till the children's dinner-time, when Mrs. Mildmay was pleased to see that she looked very much abashed on coming in to take her seat at the table, and accordingly spoke kindly to her, to encourage these symptoms of better feeling.

Next day, when the morning's play was over, and the children went into the school, Cecily followed them in.

"I can't let you stay here, my dear," said Mrs. Mildmay, "for children never attend to their lessons when another child is playing in the same room."

Cecily lingered a moment before she walked to the door, then, as if suddenly taking a resolution, she came back, saying: "I should like to learn a lesson too."

"I'm glad of that, my dear child," replied Mrs. Mildmay, "for I'm sure you'll relish your play all the better."

And then she gave her an easy little task, so as not to discourage her; for

Mrs. Mildmay guessed that Cecily had no very great mind to learn a lesson at all, but that her growing affection for her young playmates made her prefer sharing their working hours, rather than playing alone, and the good lady determined to take advantage of this, to bring her into more regular habits.

All went on very smoothly for a day or two, and the hitherto idle child began to find the advantage of occupation, and to think, like her little companions, that she did play all the better after her work; but unluckily, Cecily had taken cold on the morning she wetted her feet, by sillily giving her doll a bath, and she was soon sufficiently unwell for Mrs. Mildmay to think it prudent for her to keep her chamber. Cecily fretted at being obliged to refrain from running about the garden, and would have rebelled, only she knew it would be of no use, any more than to cry—having found from experience that neither tears nor raving made the least impression upon Mrs. Mildmay—only she grew crosser and more unmanageable every day, until at last, the measles broke out, and then she was forced, from sheer weakness, to let herself be nursed, and to become a little more tractable.

Mrs. Mildmay immediately wrote off word to her little charge's mamma, to let her know that her child was ill; at the same time advising Mrs. Wilton so strongly not to give up the benefit she was deriving from sea-bathing, for the sake of coming back to nurse Cecily —whose symptoms of the malady were exceedingly favourable, and whom she assured her should be taken every care of—that the indolent lady gladly consented to leave her in such good hands.

Mrs. Mildmay was well satisfied by her neighbour's decision: for as the child could not have been safely removed at present, even if her mamma had come home, Mrs. Wilton would, of course, have been nearly all day in the house, and, instead of helping, would only have increased Mrs. Mildmay's perplexities tenfold. If Mrs. Mildmay had already a hard struggle to contend against the obstinacy of her little patient, who at one moment would refuse to take her physic, and at another would throw off the bedclothes, when desired to keep herself warm, to what a pitch would not her unruliness have risen, if backed by the ill-judged indulgence of her weak-minded mother.

As the little Mildmays had each had the measles, and there was no danger of infection, Rosina was allowed to help her mamma and the maid in nursing their sick guest, and the amiable child did everything in her power to soothe the irritable fretfulness of the little sufferer. She would bring all her own toys to amuse her, or read stories to her; and frequently—very frequently—did she give up a pleasant walk, to remain in the sick chamber, because, she said, that "poor Cecily would think it hard that others went abroad when she could not."

Now Cecily certainly felt grateful for these marks of kindness; and the more so, perhaps, because she was secretly conscious that she would herself be incapable of such unselfish devotion towards any little playmate she might have loved ever so much. Yet her gratitude could not so entirely subdue her waywardness, but what she was continually showing her temper even to her kind little nurse.

CHAPTER V.

ONE very fine day, when Mrs. Mildmay had gone out with Algernon to make a call in the neighbourhood, and Rosina had earnestly requested to stay with Cecily, the latter took it into her head to ask for a book of costly plates, that Mrs. Mildmay had shown her a few days before, to amuse her. It was in vain Rosina told her that her mother never allowed the book to be taken out of the drawing-room, and that they never looked at it without leave. Cecily insisted on having it brought to her immediately. Rosina again repeated she would not think of touching the book in her mamma's absence, but offered to bring her all her own and Algernon's story books, and to read to her a new and pretty fairy tale she had begun yesterday.

"I don't want any of your books," replied Cecily, pettishly, "I will have the prints."

"Do be good, Cecily." (Poor Rosina said this at least twenty times a day). "You know I would bring the book you wish for if I might."

"But I will have it," said Cecily, "and I shall get up and fetch it myself, since you won't."

And she began to get out of bed.

"Cecily!" cried Rosina, holding up her tiny finger, and almost assuming the authority of womanhood, "I shall ring for Jemima, if you behave so."

"I don't care for Jemima," said Cecily; "I will do as I like."

"Indeed, you must not get out of bed, Cecily," cried Rosina, quite alarmed, "you know Jemima told you that those ugly red spots will never go away, unless you lie still and keep warm."

"I tell you I don't care a fig for Jemima—and that I hate her," shrieked Cecily, now worked up into a passion, and struggling with Rosina, who dared not leave the bedside to ring the bell, but kept trying to tuck up her boisterous charge.

She was, however, speedily relieved by hearing Jemima's cheerful and sonorous voice calling out: "A deal I care for your hates or your likes, my little Missy; but out of bed you shan't stir, while I've the care of you." And the moment after, her tall figure appeared in the frame of the open door, bearing a waiter containing a piece of cake and an ominous-looking wine-glass.

Cecily was cowed for the moment, but she turned her head away sullenly, and made believe not to see Jemima, who now approached the bedside, saying: "Here's your physic, Miss Cecily, now take it like a good child—and there's some nice cake to put out the taste."

"I won't take it," said Cecily.

"You must, Miss Cecily—that's all I shall say," replied Jemima, firmly. "Dear bless me! why *our* children never make these fusses when they are ill."

"I tell you I won't!" roared Cecily; drumming on the counterpane, with her two fists, in double quick time.

"You are not going to play off any of your tantrums on me, Miss, I can tell you," said Jemima, with sturdy calmness.

"Then take that!" retorted Cecily, giving her a box on the ear.

"O fie, Cecily, I am ashamed of you," exclaimed Rosina, colouring with indignation. "To think of striking our good Jemima, who has been so kind to you?"

Cecily showed no symptoms of repentance, and remained doggedly silent.

"You ought to ask Jemima's pardon," continued Rosina, "or I am sure mamma will make you when she comes home."

"I won't ask her pardon—and won't take the nasty physic—but I *will* have the book—and don't care for any of you," cried Cecily, and popped her head under the be-dclothes, as if she thought she was playing them a great trick, by depriving them of the sight of her little bloated face.

"She's a wicked child," said Jemima, "and doesn't deserve our doing anything for her. So I'd just leave her alone, Miss Rosina, and when your mamma comes home, I'll tell her all about it."

Jemima wanted Rosina to go away, while she would stay to watch that the child did not do herself any real mischief; but Rosina whispered that she thought if she were alone with Cis, she could persuade her into being good again; so the nurse went out of the room, though she observed that if Miss Rosina made too much of her, the young lady would only grow more wayward.

Rosina now sat down on her little chair, in a corner of the room, and began reading as quietly as if nothing had happened; judging, with a sagacity above her years, that her unmanageable playmate would come round much quicker, if she did not seem to coax her. And so it turned out. The moment Cecily heard the nurse's footsteps dying away, she peeped cautiously to see if Jemima were really gone, and then thinking, from the silence, that she was alone, completely disengaged her head from the bed-clothes. She now perceived her little friend in the corner, but finding she took no notice of her, she said, in a gentler tone than heretofore:

"Are you still there, Rozzy?"

"Yes," said Rosina, "I stayed to give you your physic,"—and she rose and took up the waiter and brought it to her.

But Cecily only seized hold of the cake instead, and began eating it.

"Now you are being naughty again," said Rosina, taking hold of her arm, "do pray take the physic first, and then you can finish the cake afterwards,"

"Let me alone," said Cecily; "I won't have the nasty stuff."

"But it is to do you good," returned Rosina.

"What's that to you?" was the ungracious reply.

Poor Rosina was hurt.

After the kindness she had laboured to bestow on her little playmate, she felt, though she could not have put it into words, that there was a degree of ingratitude in thus, as it were, calling her friendship into question, that fell like a damp upon her heart. She stepped back involuntarily, and a few tears gathered in her eyes, as she said: "How naughty of you, Cis, to say so!"

"Why, you don't love me, I'm sure," objected Cecily, "for you are always calling me naughty—and Algey doesn't love me either—nor Jemima—nor——"

Here Cecily burst into a passionate flood of tears.

"I'm sure I should love you very much," said Rosina, soothingly, "if you would but be good. And you would be such a pretty little girl too, if you always behaved well."

Rosina was obviously of the opinion of the homely saying: "Handsome is that handsome does;" and it would have been well if Cecily had been more convinced of its truth.

"But don't cry," added the kind-hearted child, "for it makes those spots on your face grow so red."

There is something so irresistible in kindness that is not to be repelled by even an ungracious return, that it finished

Cicely and Rosina.   P. 91.

The Captive Sky-lark.

by touching Cecily's stubborn though not wholly ungrateful heart, especially as she felt that Rosina bore with her temper because she was ill; well knowing that such behaviour would not be tolerated in Mrs. Mildmay's house from any but an invalid. So without saying a word, she took up the glass which Rosina was still holding on the tray, and drank off its contents.

"Now you are really a good Cecily," said Rosina, brightening up, and putting her arm round her little patient's neck.

Pleased at the sound of praise, which she so rarely deserved, Cecily smiled through the tears that were still standing on her bloated cheeks: and said, "And will you love me when I'm pretty again?"

Mrs. Mildmay just then entered the

room, on her return from her walk, carrying a beautiful nosegay in her hand. Having heard what their little guest was saying, she observed: "My dear, I am sure it would make no difference to Rosina whether you were pretty or not; and she would love you, even with those ugly spots on your face, if you were always good. But Jemima says you refused to take your physic."

Rosina crept round to her mother, and, standing on tiptoe, whispered a few words in her ear, upon which Mrs. Mildmay smiled, and said: "Well, well, since you *have* taken it, I will not say anything more about it this time. But have you been good in other respects, Cecily?"

Cecily was silent, and, as usual when

not choosing to answer, covered herself up in the bed-clothes.

Mrs. Mildmay told Rosina to go down and take a run in the garden, where she would find Algernon; and on being left alone with her troublesome little charge, she said: "Another time I shall not allow Rosina to stay with you, Cecily, since I find that you do not attend to what she says, and would have got out of bed if Jemima had not prevented you?"

Cecily now began to cry more vociferously than ever.

"Rosina gave up a nice walk," continued Mrs Mildmay, "on purpose to stay in a sick room and take care of you, which I daresay is more than you would do for her."

Struck by the obvious truth of this remark, Cecily stopped crying, and observed, with more candour than amiability: "No—I'd rather run about than be in anybody's sick room."

"Because you are selfish," said Mrs. Mildmay. "Now Rosina gives up her pleasure, and playing with her brother, all for the sake of a little ungrateful puss who refuses to lie still for her own good. Nor did we forget you, while we were out, either—for Algernon gathered these flowers, for you, because he said they would make poor Cis's room look gay; and I bought you this little box of household articles for your doll's house, at the village toy-shop you were longing so to visit the other day. And pray, what do you think we gain by being kind to you?"

Cecily again began to cry, but more silently, like one who begins to be sorry for her behaviour. At last she said: "I think I would nurse Rozzy though, if she were ill—yes, I'm sure I would. But won't you let her stay with me any more, when you go out?"

"That must depend on your own conduct, Cecily," replied Mrs. Mildmay, who suspected these fine promises arose solely from the selfish fear of being deprived of Rosina's company.

Jemima now entered the room to inform Mrs. Mildmay that dinner was ready, when Cecily hastened to say; "I will behave better next time—indeed I will—and I'll be good even to Jemima."

"You should not say *even*, Cecily,"

replied Mrs. Mildmay, "for Jemima has done more for you than any of us."

"But she's only a servant," retorted Cecily, "and I beat and pinch my nurse as often as I like, because mamma says it's her business to please me, and that she has her wages for it."

"Hush—hush, my dear; you are talking nonsense," said Mrs. Mildmay. "No wages can pay for kindness. Besides, Jemima is not your mamma's servant; nor is it her business to sit up every night with you, as she did at first when you were so ill, from her own free will, and out of pure kindness, because you were a helpless sick child.

Meanwhile Jemima had put the nosegay into a jug of water, which she placed on the window-sill, so that the smell might not affect the little invalid, but that it might cheer her sight.

"Then I'm sorry now that I slapped her face," said Cecily. "Will you forgive me, Jemima, if mamma gives you something pretty?"

Cecily thought that any affront might be redeemed by a present.

"Bless your heart!" replied Jemima, "I don't want anybody to give me anything. All I want is for you to get well. I forgive you with all my heart—for you know, Miss, we must all do as we would be done by."

Do as we would be done by! Yes, this was the watchword of Mrs. Mildmay's whole household, and a golden rule it is; for, if everybody observed it strictly, there would be no more crimes and injustice committed in the world!

Of course, it was not to be expected that Cecily could be reformed in a day, nor even in a few weeks; still, this wholesome maxim, by dint of being not merely preached, but practised by all around her, began to sink slowly, if not into her heart, at least into her mind. And one of the first evidences she gave of an improved feeling was her asking of Rosina, on her coming up-stairs again after dinner, "Who has taken care of my lark all this while?"

Rosina told her they had all taken care that he wanted for nothing.

"Suppose, Rozzy, you took some of the flowers Algernon brought me," said Cecily, "and put them round the lark's cage. Perhaps it would please him."

Rosina was just going to say : " I think it would please him much better to be let out"—when, recollecting that her mamma had told her not to interfere on this subject with Cecily, as Mrs. Mildmay wished to let the workings of the child's mind take their own course, she said she would select any flowers Cecily liked to spare, and put them round the bird's cage, which she assured her had been decked with leaves every day.

"Thank Algey for bringing me the nosegay," added Cecily, while Rosina was picking out a few of the flowers. " Oh, how I do long to run about the garden again!" added she, with a sigh.

"You soon will, Miss Cecily," observed Jemima, who sat sewing in a corner of the chamber, "if you do but keep quiet."

"Now you mustn't get out of bed, Cis, while I'm away," said Roslna, on leaving the room.

"No, I won't, Rozzy," replied Cecily, who was playing quietly with the box of little household articles which Mrs. Mildmay had given her.

CHAPTER VI.

The weather was so favourable for the little invalid's recovery, that in about a week, though still confined to the house, she was able to lie on the sofa in the drawing-room during the greater part of the day, which proved a great relief to her impatient spirit, especially as the children devoted the greater part of their playhours to endeavouring to amuse her. Algernon would read to her, or review his leaden soldiers on a table for her amusement; while Rosina would nurse the doll Cecily had spoilt, and whom she insisted on it was very ill, and then put it to bed in its cradle;, and thus the time flew so pleasantly, that when Mrs. Mildmay came to fetch the children to take a turn in the garden, before they resumed their lessons, Cecily was often ready to cry at parting with them.

One day, as they were all three playing together, Mrs. Mildmay came in and said to her children: "My dears, Mrs. Walters is below in her pony phaeton, and has come to take us to Springdale Park, where we shall have tea in one of the grottoes. Her little nieces and nephews are to join us there."

The children looked up, in high delight, and were beginning to put by their toys.

"Mustn't I go too?" whimpered Cecily.

"My dear child, you must not begin by a long ride," said Mrs Mildmay; "but the doctor said you might take a walk in the garden to-morrow."

"But to-morrow is so long to wait for!" returned Cecily.

Rosina had suddenly stopped packing up their playthings, and looked wistfully at her mother, who understood her meaning, and said: "Well, children, do you like to go? Or would you rather stay?"

"We'll stay, mamma," said they in a breath.

"But are you sure, Algernon," asked his mother, "that you will not repent the moment we have driven off—and feel sorry when you think you might have been playing at hide-and-seek with the little Forsters, or trundling hoops, and so forth?" for Mrs. Mildmay knew her boy was fond of out-door exercise, and was less sure of his staying willingly than of Rosina's making the sacrifice to their little friend.

"No, mamma," said Algernon, after a moment's hesitation, "I shall not repent —besides, I can trundle my hoop here in the garden."

"Then, good bye, dear children," said Mrs. Mildmay, kissing them both, and much pleased with their readiness to give up their amusement for a sick companion's sake; and taking leave of Cecily, she went to join Mrs. Walters and drove off.

"It is very kind of you to stay with me," said Cecily, to whom such abnegation appeared past comprehension; "I wonder how you would, when your mamma said you might go."

"Why," said Rosina, cheerfully, "mamma always tells us to do as we would be done by; so Algey and I thought you wouldn't like to be left alone."

"I'll give you any of my playthings you like," cried Cecily, in a fit of generosity excited by so good an example. "And we shall all play so nicely together, when I'm well, for I mean to be good," added she, with the pretty candour of her age.

When Mrs. Mildmay came back, she told the children that Mrs. Walters was so pleased to hear Rosina and Algernon had stayed at home on account of their little friend, that she invited them all, as soon as Cecily should be well, to spend the day at a farm-house she possessed, a good many miles off, in the neighbourhood of a forest, where they should dine on the grass, and have strawberries and cream in the evening.

O how pleased were the children to think they had done what was right and kind, and to have now before them the prospect of such a delightful day! Why, it was a pleasure even to talk about it beforehand, and to conjecture what the farm-house was like, and how much larger the forest might be, than their own little wood beyond the garden.

Nor was it long they had to wait before their wishes were realised. Cecily mended rapidly when once it was safe for her to run about the garden as heretofore, and with the return of health, her temper improved, feeling as she now did, the necessity of checking any outbursts of passion or wilfulness, towards those who had been so unvarying in their kindness during the tedious hours of illness. The three children, therefore, got on very comfortably together, and Cecily had left off saying: "I won't play!" even if her companions did not give in to all her whims, and began to understand that she must yield sometimes, if she wished others to yield to her.

Well! the much wished-for day came at last, and our little folks were on the tiptoe of expectation, when the pony-phaeton at last drove up to the door, to fetch them away to the farm, where they were to meet Mrs. Walters.

Just as they were going to set off, Cecily looked up into Mrs. Mildmay's face, saying: "May I take my lark with me, Mrs. Mildmay?"

"Yes, my dear," replied the lady.

"What for, Cis?" asked Algernon.

"Never mind, Algey," said Mrs. Mildmay, seeing that Cecily did not seem to like being questioned. "I have no objection to Cecily's giving him a ride, provided the cage is held steadily, and not knocked about."

"I'll hold it on my lap," said Cecily.

They then stepped into the phaeton, and drove through the pretty green lanes, that looked delightfully fresh at that early hour, amidst the twittering of the birds on the boughs, and the sweet smells from the flowering hedges.

Algernon was in bounding spirits, while Rosina, though quieter, was in quite as enjoying a mood; indeed, having been so frequently detained at home of late, by her kind offices as nurse, the country had never, in all her little life, seemed so delightful to her as on that particular morning. As to Cecily, she was evidently pleased likewise, albeit she appeared to be brooding over something or other in her own mind; for, though one moment she would rattle on very gaily, by-and-by she would look at her lark, and call him by some endearing term, and then grow pensive. But what it was all about, the children did not take the trouble to guess, though their mamma surmised it.

At last they reached the farm-house, where Mrs. Walters received them very kindly; and, kissing the little Mildmays, told them she was pleased to hear what good children they were, and that she hoped they would spend a very pleasant day, to make up for their not accompanying their mamma last time.

"Kiss me, too," said Cecily, holding up her little cheek, "because I mean to be good."

"I am glad to hear it, my pretty little girl," said good-natured Mrs. Walters, exchanging a smile with Mrs. Mildmay, while she embraced Cecily most heartily.

After partaking of some refreshments, and looking over the nicely-kept farm, they once more stepped into the phaeton, and drove off to the forest, with a large basket containing all the requisites for a cold dinner.

The forest was indeed vastly different to the little wood at the bottom of the garden—it was so large that it looked as if one might easily get lost in it. They now alighted from the carriage to walk under the wide-spreading trees, and to choose a nice place for dinner.

"You had better leave the cage in the phaeton, my dear," said Mrs. Walters, perceiving that Cecily was carrying it with her.

A few weeks back Cecily would have answered rudely: "No, I won't"—but now she said, "I want to take it, please ma'am."

"Suppose we hang it on a tree till we come back?" said Algernon, "for you can't run with the cage in your hand, Cis."

But Cecily turned away from him as if that did not suit her either.

"What are you going to do with him, Cecily?" asked the little boy.

"I am going to do as I'd be done by," said Cecily, with an emphasis that was quite amusing in her infantine voice.

Mrs. Walters was going to make some inquiry, when a sign from Mrs. Mildmay caused her to refrain, and the two ladies let the children walk on before, and follow their own devices.

They had now reached a lovely spot, where the trees were arching over head like the aisles of a cathedral, when Cecily, who had hitherto remained silent, suddenly cried out: "Here goes!" and opened the cage, adding, "Good bye, my dear, pretty lark!"

Out the bird fluttered, half timidly at first, as if he doubted either his good luck or his strength after his long captivity, and perched upon a bough. There he began twittering to try his voice, and arranging his feathers as if for a long journey—next he hopped from tree to tree till he caught a glimpse of the sky above, when, gathering courage from his new-found liberty—up—up he soared, pouring forth a torrent of liquid melody that sounded like a hymn of gratitude to his little deliverer.

Cecily watched him with eager eyes till he was completely beyond all human sight, and then, dashing away a tear with her natural petulance, said: "I don't suppose he'll ever come back."

"He'll not be such a fool as that, Cis," said Algernon, laughing. "But do you repent?"

"Oh no, no!" cried Cecily, "I won't repent, for that would be wrong, wouldn't it?"

Rosina fell upon her neck. "You can't think how glad I am!" said she; "this was what I wished you to do all along. I love you now, Cis, so very much!"

Mrs. Mildmay now joined the children, and patted Cecily's cheek, saying: "That's right, my dear child; now I have good hopes of you."

And Cecily felt very proud of Mrs. Mildmay's approbation; and, for the first time in her life, perceived there was something sweeter to the heart than she could have imagined in doing a good action, though it was only to a poor dumb creature.

The children spent the day very happily, and none were so gay and so blithe as Cecily, whom Mrs. Walters declared to have quite redeemed her promise of becoming good.

Shortly after this memorable event in Cecily's childish existence, her mamma returned home from the sea-side, and was delighted to find her child not only grown, and improved in outward appearance, but become sufficiently mindful of others to avoid all boisterous play and pettish outbreaks, whenever Mrs. Wilton was resting on the sofa, or had a headache. Cecily remembered how the Mildmays had behaved to her, and on such occasions a still small voice would whisper to her: "Do as you would be done by!" At first, indeed, Cecily followed this good maxim merely as a habit, but afterwards she grew to consider it as a duty, and at last it became a pleasure to her.

"Oh! how much I owe to your kindness and wise management, my dear Mrs. Mildmay!" said Mrs. Wilton, with tears in her eyes, to that amiable lady—"Pray let us never lose sight of each other, and complete the good work you have begun by letting Cecily continue to associate with your children as often as possible."

To facilitate this desirable object, Mrs. Wilton ever after spent part of the year in London, and generally invited the Mildmays to spend some weeks during the summer at her house, instead of hiring the cottage next door, so that the intimacy continued between the children, and Cecily was prevented by the frequent presence of good example, from relapsing into her former wilful ways.

And, now, should any of our little readers inquire whether Cecily ever regretted having given the lark his liberty, we can safely say that she did not. For a long time after, as often as she heard the larks singing over her head, she would say: "I wonder whether *my* lark is among them?" But this was only because she liked to fancy he was enjoying himself, and all through her doing. Nor to this day can she ever listen to their charming choir without a pleasurable sensation arising from the consciousness that she had done what was right, on that particular occasion (and perhaps for the first time in her life from disinterested motives)—nor without a lively sense of gratitude to Mrs. Mildmay for having taught her, by the best and most impressive means, to "Do as she would be done by."

THE END.

CPSIA information can be obtained at www.ICGtesting.com
Printed in the USA
BVOW05s1415160316

440585BV00007B/21/P